Children are Struggling in this New World

Children are Struggling in this New World

The challenges that pre-teens and teens are faced with, their causes and effects, and what parents, guardians, teachers, and others can do to help them

Stephanie E. Nichols

Published by Zone 4 Kids

An imprint of Tamarind Hill Press Limited

Newton Aycliffe, County Durham, DL5 6XP

14023099

ISBN Print: 978-1-915161-99-4

ISBN eBook: 978-1-915161-98-7

Copyright © Stephanie E. Nichols 2022

All rights reserved. No part of this book may be reproduced or used in any manner without the prior written permission of the copyright owner, except for the use of brief quotations in a book review.

The advice and strategies found within may not be suitable for every situation. This work is sold with the understanding that neither the author nor the publisher is held responsible for the results accrued from the advice in this book. The book is not sold with the intention of providing any service to the reader.

Disclaimer: This book must not serve as or replace legal nor professional advice from a counsellor, psychologist, therapist, etc. It is the reader's responsibility to seek professional help where necessary.

Table of Contents

About the Author 7

Introduction 8

Cyberbullying 10

    What is Cyberbullying? 10

    What are the Causes of Cyberbullying? 12

    The Effects of Cyberbullying on Children and Teenagers 16

    Who Children can Talk to if they are being Cyberbullied 24

    How can Cyberbullying Affect their Adult Lives Later? 26

    Stories About Cyberbullying - Examples 27

    How to Deal with Cyberbullying 29

    How can Children Heal from Cyberbullying? 30

    BULLYING AND CYBERBULLYING HELP 32

Eating Disorders 33

    What are Eating Disorders? 33

    What are the Causes of Eating Disorders? 34

    The Effects of Eating Disorders 39

    Who Children should Talk to when Experiencing Eating Disorders 43

    How can Eating Disorders Affect their Adult Lives Later? 45

    Stories about Eating Disorders 46

    How to Deal with Eating Disorders 48

    How can Children Heal from Eating Disorders? 50

    EATING DISORDERS HELP 51

Child Abuse 52

    What is Child Abuse? 52

    What are the Causes of Child Abuse? 55

    The Effects of Child Abuse 57

    Who Children should Talk to when Experiencing Child Abuse 61

How can Child Abuse Affect their Adult Lives Later? 62
Stories about Child Abuse 64
How to Deal with Child Abuse 66
How can Children Heal from Child Abuse? 69
CHILD ABUSE HELP 71
Low Self-Esteem 72
   What is Self-Esteem? 72
   What are the Causes of Low Self-Esteem? 74
   The Effects of Low Self-esteem 76
   Who Children Should Talk to When Experiencing Low Self-Esteem 77
   How can Low Self-esteem Affect their Adult Lives Later? 78
   Stories about Low Self-Esteem 80
   How to Deal with Low Self-Esteem 81
   How can Children Heal from Low Self-Esteem? 83
   LOW SELF-ESTEEM HELP 84
Social Pressure 85
   What is Social Pressure? 85
   The Causes of Children Giving in to Social Pressure 87
   The Effects of Peer/Social Pressure 91
   Who Children should Talk to When Experiencing Social Pressure 93
   How can Social Pressure Affect their Adult Lives Later? 94
   Stories about Social Pressure 95
   How to Deal with Social Pressure 97
   How can Children Heal from Social Pressure? 98
   SOCIAL PRESSURE HELP 99

About the Author

Stephanie E. Nichols is a wife and mother of two teenagers. She is also a grade-school teacher and Bible School teacher. She has influenced many young people both in her career and personal life and continues to do so today. Raised by both parents who were very involved in her upbringing, Stephanie understands the part that played in her happiness both as a child and an adult. When asked about how she dealt with the challenges she faced as a teenager, Stephanie points out that it was through the talks and help of her parents that she was able to deal with things like bullying and even her first broken heart.

In raising her own children, being in a close-knit family where she knows what goes on with the children in it, and through her career, Stephanie realises that children indeed have a lot to deal with in today's world. As a mother, Stephanie has had to help her children work through some of these challenges and now wants to extend some advice to the rest of the world, so that parents and guardians can help their children navigate the changing world.

Introduction

Life is full of challenges and worries, no matter your age. From an adult viewpoint, a child or teenager's life may appear to be nothing but blissful. Truth is, though, being a child/teenager doesn't exempt you from experiencing difficulties or having to face complex life challenges.

It's not easy growing up. And today's children face a wide variety of problems that might cause fear and anxiety, depending on their circumstances. Consequently, it's no surprise that many adolescents endure significant challenges as they transition from infancy to adulthood and sometimes react by either acting out or shutting the world out.

A child is a sweet, innocent creature at birth, who's full of potential and promise. However, there are several forces ready to overwhelm and weaken them. The scope and severity of the issues that children encounter is troubling. If we left things to happen to our children without giving them the right tools to face them, we will raise broken adults who struggle to navigate the world.

It is critical to recognize and address what our children are going through as soon as possible. This way, we are able to limit or even reverse the impact it will have on them. It gives us an opportunity to aid in their development and progress into adulthood.

This book discusses the causes and effects of children experiencing cyberbullying, eating disorders, child abuse, low self-esteem, and social pressure. It looks into how children can cope and heal from these challenges.

Depending on the age and capability of the child, you may leave them to read the book on their own or decide to undergo the process with them. While one may not be dealing with all the challenges discussed in the book, I recommend reading through each chapter and learning as much as you can from them. It gives you the opportunity to know how to handle these issues if they come up in the future or how to help a friend in need.

Each chapter in the book provides real-life examples to better explain what was discussed. At the end of each chapter, I have added at least one resource for those dealing with the problem. Parents, guardian, and even children themselves can seek help from the resources listed. Sometimes, help is only a phone call away.

I hope that you find this book useful and that it may help you, your child, or someone you know.

Cyberbullying

With the growth of the Internet and the online world, we have seen a major shift in the way people socialise. Nowadays, children build relationships online with people they do not know or take their real-life friendships online—being friends on different social media platforms, for example—and just like in real life, a lot can happen there. One of the biggest problems that we have seen between children and teenagers today is cyberbullying, which is what we will discuss in this chapter.

By the end of the chapter, you will understand what constitutes cyberbullying, the causes and effects, and what to do if you experience this problem.

Note: As you read, you might begin to realise that a negative behaviour or set of behaviours you yourself portray is cyberbullying. Though this book does not go into that, my hope is that you will understand the effects it has and refrain from continuing that behaviour.

What is Cyberbullying?

Cyberbullying is an aggressive, cruel, or intimidating action directed towards another person over the internet. Unlike "regular" bullying, which occurs in person, cyberbullying occurs online and can potentially be considered a kind of cybercrime. However, it is very similar to bullying in that the perpetrator wants to be in control and targets those who are *weaker*—power imbalance is always present. The cyber bully assumes this authority to harass and weaken his or her victims.

Cyberbullying can take many different forms. The following are just a few examples of how it can play out/unfold online:

1. Sharing an embarrassing video of someone on social media sites, such as Facebook or video-sharing websites such as YouTube.

2. Sending offensive, threatening, or improper texts or images.

3. Posting private information about others online.

4. Sharing a person's photo and personal information without their permission.

5. Making derogatory remarks about another user on a forum.

6. Disseminating false information about a person online.

7. "Happy slapping," which is the act of recording and sharing videos of abusive attacks.

8. Creating a fake profile on social media platforms in order to make fun of or harm someone's reputation.

9. Sending others threatening or obscene letters and emails.

10. Harassing someone in a chat room on a regular basis.

11. Excluding someone from a social networking group on purpose.

12. Forcibly obtaining personal information about an individual in order to use it against him or her.

What are the Causes of Cyberbullying?

Children bully each other online for a variety of reasons. To understand cyberbullying and how it affects children, it is important to identify the platforms that enable cyberbullies to thrive.

Technology is wonderful, but it does allow some gaps through which particular deviant behaviour might manifest. Cyberbully victims are targeted in a variety of ways.

The ease with which anyone can be found and contacted via social media worsens the problem. Children now have unprecedented access to a vast amount of knowledge and millions of individuals through the internet. This is risky because, while most children deal with bullying at school, they now have to also face it at home. In addition, it's no longer just other kids who go after them.

Social media pages, instant messaging and direct messaging apps, and forums are where you will find the most culprits. Such platforms have rules that govern behaviour, but they can't monitor every chat. And because privacy is an issue, most people get away with it if they aren't reported.

To put an end to online bullying, however, you must first comprehend why children engage in it. Their reasons for venting in cyberspace can range from rage and vengeance to a desire to fit in. So, what are the causes of cyberbullying?

Revenge

When children are bullied, they often pursue revenge rather than dealing with the situation in a healthier manner. They decide that retaliation is the best way to deal with the hurt they have suffered. These children are commonly referred to as bully-victims when this occurs. Bully-victims justify their behaviour by claiming that they, too, have been hounded and tortured.

They want others to feel the same way they do, and they believe they have a right to do so. They may also feel relieved and vindicated for what they have gone through by cyberbullying others. These kids will go after their bully directly on occasion. They may also target someone they regard to be weaker or more vulnerable than themselves.

It's the Victim's Fault

Bullying is often motivated by a person's social standing at school. Because of the school's social hierarchy, some students will cyberbully others. For example, an anonymous group of girls may cyberbully a mean girl in the hopes of humbling or humiliating her. In another instance, a classmate who excels academically may be cyberbullied by a mean girl who is jealous of her achievement. A child may also cyberbully a peer if they fear the victim has stolen their crush or their partner. For whatever reason, some children believe their cyberbullying is justified and deserved. As a result, they are rarely remorseful or guilty about cyberbullying.

Boredom

Yes, it can be that simple! Kids who are bored and looking for amusement will occasionally turn to cyberbullying to spice up their life with some excitement and drama. They may also opt to cyberbully due to a lack of parental attention and supervision. Therefore, the Internet serves as both a source of amusement and a means of gaining attention for them.

Peer Pressure

To blend in with a group of friends or a clique, children will sometimes engage in cyberbullying.

Consequently, in trying to gain acceptance at school, some children surrender to peer pressure, even if it means acting against their better judgment.

These bullies are more concerned about social acceptance than the consequences of cyberbullying. You'll find that groups or cliques have this false sense of security in numbers, so they will engage in cyberbullying together.

Everyone is doing it

When kids are of the belief that a lot of individuals are bullying online, they are more inclined to participate in the same behaviour. Because their peer group approves of the behaviour, it doesn't seem as serious of an issue to them. Furthermore, to fit in with a group that regularly harasses others online, children will cyberbully others.

Power

Cyberbullying can be a reflection of one's social standing. Those who are popular frequently make fun of others who are not as popular. Similarly, attractive children may single out those they consider to be unattractive. The Internet becomes a weapon used to spread relational aggression and mean behaviour.

They may also use cyberbullying to propagate stories and gossip, as well as ostracize others. On the other hand, children trying to climb the social ladder at school or obtain social power will use cyberbullying to get attention. They may also cyberbully to lower another person's social position. Cyberbullies have a variety of objectives, but the overarching goal is to strengthen their own power by weakening someone else's.

Lack of Empathy

The majority of children who engage in cyberbullying believe that it is not a big deal. They have little or no guilt for their actions because they are oblivious to the pain they inflict on others. In fact, multiple studies have indicated that many children who engage in online bullying have no empathy for the victims after the bullying has occurred. Instead, several children said that online bullying made them laugh, feel popular, and feel powerful.

The Effects of Cyberbullying on Children and Teenagers
Bullying can have both physical and psychological effects on a child. Low self-esteem, depression, anxiety, fear, behavioural problems, and academic issues are just a few of the difficulties that children may face if they are targeted. Cyberbullying, on the other hand, can be even more harmful.

This could be due to a number of factors. While traditional bullying is limited to the spaces in which it can take place (school, church, neighbourhood park, etc.) and when it does (at school, usually in the daytime), cyberbullying is not. It can happen anywhere through the internet and at any time of the day. In traditional bullying, the perpetrator/bully is usually known by the person being bullied; they can see them face-to-face. This is not the case for cyberbullying where one can be bullied without knowing exactly by who. This makes it more ruthless and, in some cases, more difficult to resolve.

The intensity of the effects of victimization might vary depending on the type of victimization. One study indicated that harassment delivered through text messages or phone calls was more detrimental than that of online photos and posts.

The effects of cyberbullying can be broken down into various categories as shown below:

Emotional Effects of Cyberbullying

A victim of cyberbullying may experience the following emotional effects:

1. **Humiliation/Embarrassment**

Children who are harassed or teased online have the constant feeling that their content is out in the open and exposed to the world. They know that once it's out there, it will always be out there, and that it cannot be unseen or erased. As a result, children feel embarrassed and humiliated not just in front of their peers and friends, but also in front of the entire world. This makes the embarrassment greater, simply because more people are witness to it.

2. Isolation

Cyberbullying can lead to children being excluded and ostracized in school. As a result, they often feel alone and isolated. You find that children also shun social interaction. As a part of growing up, children need to socialise and be part of groups. They need friends, so being isolated in this way can have devastating impacts. By being isolated, it can also affect their real-world experiences. If they do not have friends at school for example, the likelihood of them being bullied is greater.

When a child is subjected to cyberbullying, parents may advise turning off the computer or turning off their mobile devices. However, for many children, using these devices is the most significant means of communication. Turning them off typically means cutting them off from the rest of the world, making them feel even more isolated.

3. Anger

Many victims of cyberbullying will become angry with what's happening to them. In fact, research shows that the most prevalent reaction to cyberbullying is anger (followed by being upset and worried).

Victimized children may plan to get revenge and take retaliatory action. Apart from the potential trouble that they may get into, taking this route is risky since it can trap them in the bully-victim cycle.

While it is generally preferable to forgive a bully rather than seek revenge, this is often easier said than done. If your child is enraged by cyberbullying, he or she may benefit from speaking with a counsellor or therapist who can teach them how to channel their anger in constructive ways.

4. Powerlessness

Cyberbullying victims often have a difficult time feeling safe. Because cyberbullying can cause them to be isolated for example, their sense of vulnerability increases. Cyberbullying can seep into any space they occupy—like their home—at any time, leaving them feeling helpless. This reduces their ability to feel safe anywhere. In essence, cyberbullying can feel like it's all around you if you're a victim.

Furthermore, because the bullies can stay anonymous, this understanding may intensify their fear. Although some cyberbullies pick people they know and have no issue identifying themselves, some children who are targeted may have no idea who is causing them harm.

Mental Effects of Cyberbullying

Victims who are continuously experiencing cyberbullying may have a different relationship with the world than others. Life can feel hopeless and meaningless for many children who suffer from cyberbullying.

They may lose interest in activities they once enjoyed and spend less time connecting with family and friends. In certain circumstances, depression and suicidal thoughts may develop.

A. Depression and Anxiety

Cyberbullying victims are more likely to develop anxiety, depression, and other stress-related illnesses. The additional stress of having to deal with cyberbullying on a regular basis can take away their joy and fulfilment. It can also make them feel more worried and isolated.

Cyberbullying can destroy one's self-esteem and self-worth, which can lead to depression and anxiety.

Increased levels of cyberbullying have regularly been linked to increased levels of depression, according to research. They may experience feelings of hopelessness, sadness, and powerlessness.

B. Low Self-Esteem

Cyberbullying often focuses on the aspects of victims' lives that make them feel most vulnerable. For example, a child who is self-conscious about their weight may be bullied because of it.

Even if this isn't the case, internet bullying can have a negative impact on one's self-esteem. Bullying victims may develop a deep dissatisfaction with who they are and whether they have value. They may feel a lack of self-worth.

Cyberbullying, according to researchers, may induce psychological maladjustment, lower well-being, and eventually low self-esteem in children, especially teenagers.

C. Academic Issues

Children who are victims of cyberbullying may lose interest in school. Consequently, they often have considerably higher absenteeism rates than non-bullied children. They may miss school to avoid having to face their cyberbullies or because the messages they received were too embarrassing and humiliating. They will find it difficult to concentrate whether in school or during their homework sessions, which will cause their grades to suffer. For some kids, it may be as extreme leading to them dropping out of school or not pursuing higher education—they want to leave the schooling system as soon as possible.

D. Suicidal Thoughts and Self-Harm

Targets of cyberbullying have been known to harm themselves in some way in response to the intense feelings they experience. Some children, especially teenagers for example, may self-harm by slashing or burning themselves. Numerous studies have shown how cyberbullying and self-harm are related.

Cyberbullying increases the risk of suicide. Kids who are frequently bullied by their peers via text messages, instant messaging, social media, or apps may feel hopeless and believe that the only way to stop the misery is to commit suicide.

As a result, individuals may fantasize about dying to get away.

Behavioural Effects of Cyberbullying

For those bullied online, their behavioural changes may be the same as those who are bullied in the traditional way. You will find that they have less interest in some of the activities they would usually enjoy. Additionally, they may become secretive.

In extreme circumstances, especially when cyberbullying goes on for a long period of time, children's behaviour might change dramatically.

These can include the following:

I. **Drug or Alcohol Abuse**

Children who are bullied online are more prone to abuse drugs or alcohol. In fact, one study indicated that cyberbully victims were 2.5 times more likely than their friends to use marijuana or binge drink.

II. **Truancy**

Going to school, especially if their schoolmates know about the bullying, can be very difficult for the victim. As a result, it's not uncommon for children to skip school or act in ways that result in suspension.

III. **Carrying a Weapon**

Children who experience cyberbullying may feel compelled to take revenge on their bully, so they bring a weapon to school.

Physical Effects of Cyberbullying

Being the subject of cyberbullying can be extremely devastating, especially if a large number of children are involved. Overwhelm and stress can appear physiologically, resulting in concerns such as:

1) Gastrointestinal issues

Irritable bowel syndrome, abdominal pain, and stomach ulcers can all be exacerbated or caused by the stress of bullying. Children may also experience nausea, vomiting, and diarrhoea on a regular basis.

2) Disordered eating

When children experience cyberbullying, their eating habits may change, such as missing meals or binge eating. Because they feel that they cannot control what is going on in their lives as a result of the bullying, they try to control one of the only things they feel that they can—their eating. These efforts can turn into an eating disorder, especially if the bullying has left them with a distorted body image.

3) Sleep disturbances

When being cyberbullied, because the victim does not know when the person(s) will attack and have no control over it, their sleeping pattern can also be affected negatively. You might find that they get frequent nightmares, struggle to fall asleep at nights, or even begin to sleep excessively.

Who Children can Talk to if they are being Cyberbullied

Children should seek assistance by informing an adult about being cyberbullied. Telling someone may sound daunting, but it will not only get the child support, but it will also make them feel less afraid. They should bring the printed threats to their parents if they are being threatened online. The parents should notify their local police station's cyber-crimes unit. If their town is tiny and their police department does not have a cyber-crimes unit, they should bring the posts to the next precinct's supervising law enforcement officer.

If the child is unable to speak with their parents, they can seek help from a trustworthy teacher, guidance counsellor, or school psychologist.

If the child already told their parents and they haven't taken action, they can try telling someone else. They can confide in a close family member of theirs, a counsellor, or a favourite teacher. They would tell them exactly what occurred, when it happened, how long it's been going on, and how they're feeling.

Asking their teacher, guidance counsellor, or school psychologist what they will do to assist to stop the cyberbullying when they inform them is very important. It is their responsibility to keep the child secure. The majority of adults are concerned about bullying and will do all possible to assist the child. The child should continue to speak up and tell adults until someone comes to their aid.

How can Cyberbullying Affect their Adult Lives Later?
Cyberbullying has been shown in studies to have long-term effects. Individuals who have positive relationships with their parents and a strong support system at home will be less affected by cyberbullies in their lives, whereas those who are not surrounded by support will suffer the consequences of bullying far into adulthood. Adults who were bullied as children experience a variety of issues, including distrust, poor social skills, and a difficulty to sustain positive connections.

Cyberbullying has far-reaching consequences. Even if a bully is no longer present in a child's life, the damage he or she has caused can be irreversible. Because children are so impressionable throughout their formative years, what their peers say and do can have a long-term impact on them. When a child is subjected to daily insulting remarks, he or she may begin to believe them. It's difficult to predict how one incident or a dozen incidents will affect a child later on in their life.

Cyberbullying victims may develop a fear of being attacked or criticized at any time, and they may begin to wonder who they may trust in many interpersonal interactions. Even after the abuse ends, individuals may live in fear and expectation, anticipating the next time they're going to receive a message attacking them or some embarrassing photo of them being posted online. This mix of anxious and restless feelings can make it difficult for victims to concentrate at school and they may carry over these practices into their adult life at work, leading to poor performance.

Children who experience cyberbullying may have difficulty forming reciprocal, trusting friendships and relationships in their adult lives. The experiences that people have as children shape them into the adults that they become. As a result, it's unsurprising that the consequences of bullying can last long into adulthood. This, therefore, has an impact on their future thinking, as well as how they perceive themselves and others.

Stories About Cyberbullying - Examples
Jealousy Leads to Bullying

Mary-Anne is a shy 13-year-old who does extremely well in school and is well-behaved. She has been best friends with Simone ever since kindergarten. One day, Simone receives a text message accusing Mary-Anne of shoplifting a blouse from a department store. Simone knows this can't be true, as she spends most of her time reading and completing her homework.

The text is sent to everyone in her eight-grade math class. It turns out one of Mary-Anne's classmate was jealous that she received excellent grades all the time and all the teachers liked her, so, she spread this rumour about her. Simone persuades Mary-Anne to inform her parents and she tells her mom. Her mother encourages her to obtain copies of the text from her friends as proof in case the situation persists.

When the bullying went into the next week, her mother reported it to the school. The bully's parents were brought in by the principal. Everyone worked as a team to resolve this. The girl apologised to Mary-Anne and stopped bullying her online.

Posting on Social Media

Alex who is 15 years old, "friended" a guy on Facebook, who he had only met once at a poetry slam but didn't know well. The guy began uploading strange photos to Alex's page. Alex sent the guy a private message, requesting him to stop. However, the inappropriate posts continued. Alex sent him another message telling him to stop and that if he didn't, he would report him.

The guy continued to post and started adding posts about Alex wanting to hurt himself because his father was abusing him. Alex decided to "unfriend" the person on Facebook, block the person from his account, and reported the offensive photos to Facebook administrators. He also told his father of the things that were said about him and his father reported it to the police. Alex never heard from the guy again and the police never found out who it was.

Now that you understand more about cyberbullying and its impact, let's look at how to deal with it.

How to Deal with Cyberbullying

For some parents, cyberbullying is obvious because their child may show them a text, tweet, or comment on Instagram, or another social media platform that is blatantly nasty or harsh. It may not be as clear at other times.

When it comes to cyberbullying, there is no way to avoid being harassed. Bullying can happen at any time of day or night, so there is no respite after the school day is done. Adolescents spend a lot of time on social media, checking their accounts and sending messages, tweets, and images. This allows a bully to approach the teen at any time.

When it comes to cyberbullying, many teenagers are hesitant to notify others. This could be due to their shame of being bullied or their embarrassment at what the bully is saying. Teens may also be concerned that their parents will take away their phone or device, which is their life for the majority of them.

So, what should you do if your child is cyberbullied?

1. First, offer support to them. Make it clear to your child that they are not to blame for being bullied.

2. Speak with teachers, principals, or guidance counsellors at their school. Inform them of the bullying, especially if another student is involved.

3. Block the bully. Although they can be relentless, constantly finding ways to attack, it is always important that the child blocks them from contacting them. This means, blocking them from social media, incoming phone calls, text messaging, emailing—anywhere they can and/or have made contact.

4. Avoid responding. Remind your child not to respond to the bully's words or photographs.

5. Make a copy of the bully's comments and messages or take a screenshot of them. This can be used as proof in the future if necessary.

6. Put parental control software in place. This will allow you to view all text messages as well as online activity remotely.

How can Children Heal from Cyberbullying?
When a child is bullied, the road to healing may be more difficult than you think. The effects of cyberbullying, in fact, can last long after the bullying has stopped. Cyberbullying can also produce problems for the child later in life if it is not addressed right away.

There are numerous critical things you must do in order for your child to recover from cyberbullying. These involve not only altering your children's perceptions of the situation, but also their perceptions of themselves after being cyberbullied.

You want to make sure that your child's experience with cyberbullying does not define them. Instead, they should concentrate on what they've learned and their long-term goals. To begin, your child must acknowledge what occurred but not dwell on it. Instead, children should concentrate on taking care of themselves and growing as individuals.

It's also crucial to assist your child in coming to terms with the situation. And, as strange as it may seem, forgiving the cyberbully goes a long way toward freeing your child of the trauma. Remind them that revenge will not make them happy. Instead, individuals should let go of what happened to them and concentrate on the aspects of their lives that they can control.

Having a counsellor assist your child with their recovery may speed up the healing process. For recommendations on who to contact in your region, talk to your child's paediatrician.

Children should not downplay or minimize the severity of what has happened to them. They should be honest with themself about the pain they've been through.

Parents, guardians, family members or any adult that is helping them must also prioritize their recovery. A counsellor can assist them in making sense of their emotions and moving past the cyberbullying experience. The counsellor can also assist them in re-framing their thoughts and helping them regain control of their life.

While it may be hard to think about the bullying they experience, it is better to confront the problem head-on. Children will be on their way to healing once they accept what happened and change their perspective on themself and others.

It might take a while. So, children should be patient with themself. With a little effort, however, they'll be well on their way to a healthier mindset.

BULLYING AND CYBERBULLYING HELP

1- **STOP BULLYING NOW HOTLINE (USA)**

   CALL: 1-800-273-8255

2- **KIDS HELP PHONE (CANADA)**
   CALL: 1-800-668-6868
   TEXT: 686868

3- **CHILDLINE (UK)**
   CALL: 0800 1111

4- **NSPCC HELPLINE (UK)**
   CALL: 0808 800 5000

Eating Disorders

One of the things that gets me, is the number of children usually posting under YouTube videos about weight loss. I have seen comments from children as young as nine asking about specific diets promising to lose 15kgs in two weeks.

The idea of what we should look like as human beings is so widespread and, unfortunately, even our children are affected. So many of them want to be thinner, have wider hips, be more muscular and so on. They sometimes go to any extent to achieve their desired look and this often results in them developing eating disorders. In this chapter, we will look into this issue.

At the end of the chapter, you will find numbers that your child or teenager can call to get help. If you are in a country not mentioned in that section, try to find out what kind of help is available to you locally.

What are Eating Disorders?

Eating disorders are behavioural problems marked by significant and persistent changes in eating habits, as well as distressing thoughts and emotions. They can be extremely serious illnesses that disrupt physical, psychological, and social functioning.

Eating disorders affect up to 5% of the population and are most prevalent throughout adolescence and young adulthood. Several, particularly anorexia nervosa and bulimia nervosa, are more prevalent in women, but they can afflict anyone at any age.

Eating disorders are frequently linked to food, weight, or shape obsessions, as well as anxiety about eating or the effects of eating certain foods. Restrictive eating or avoidance of particular foods, binge eating, purging by vomiting or laxative overuse, and compulsive exercise are all behaviours connected with eating disorders. Any of them can look like addiction.

Anorexia nervosa, bulimia nervosa, binge eating disorder, avoidant restrictive food intake disorder, other specified feeding and eating disorder, pica, and rumination disorder are examples of eating disorders.

What are the Causes of Eating Disorders?

The exact cause of eating disorders is unknown. As with other mental illnesses, there may be many causes. It is believed that there is a mix of biological, behavioural, and social factors at play. The promotion of thin (sometimes unhealthy) bodies by society and social media can also play a role, especially for teenagers. And to fully understand the causes of eating disorders, we have to look at each individually. The three major ones are anorexia nervosa, bulimia nervosa, and binge eating disorder so we will look at them here:

Anorexia Nervosa

What is anorexia nervosa?

Anorexia nervosa is a form of self-starvation. This health issue causes a distorted body image in children and teenagers. They believe they are overweight, and so they significantly restrict their food intake. It also leads them to other additional behaviours that prevent them from gaining weight.

There are two types of anorexia:

The Restrictor Type. The amount of food consumed by children with this type is highly restricted. This often comprises high-carbohydrate and high-fat foods.

Bulimic (binging and purging) Type. Children binge eat and then force themselves to vomit. They may also take heavy doses of laxatives.

What causes anorexia nervosa in children?

According to experts, there are no known causes of anorexia nervosa. It usually begins with frequent dieting. However, it gradually progresses to excessive and unhealthy weight loss.

Nevertheless, factors that may contribute to anorexia include:

1. Social perceptions of physical appearance
2. Family influences
3. Chemical imbalances in the brain
4. Developmental problems
5. Distress
6. Feelings of helplessness
7. Low self-esteem
8. History of eating disorders in the family
9. A strong desire to achieve perfection
10. Feeling compelled to be skinny
11. Mood disorders such as anxiety or obsessional tendencies
12. Abuse of a child, either emotionally or sexually
13. Other mental health disorders

Children with anorexia nervosa are more likely to come from families with a history of weight problems, physical illnesses, and other mental health issues, such as depression or substance abuse. You'll find that children with this eating disorder also come from strict and critical homes. Parents might be overprotective and invasive.

Bulimia Nervosa

What is bulimia nervosa?

A child with a bulimia nervosa disorder binges or overeats uncontrollably. Self-induced vomiting can occur after overeating (purging).

A child who binges consumes far more food in a short period of time than would normally be consumed (often less than 2 hours). Binging takes place at least twice a week for a period of three months. It's possible that it may occur multiple times a day.

There are two types of bulimia:

The Purging Type: This involves regular binging and then causing themselves to vomit. Alternatively, the child may abuse laxatives, diuretics, enemas, or other bowel-clearing medications.

Non-purging Type: Instead of purging after bingeing, a child with this disorder adopts other unhealthy behaviours to maintain weight control. He or she may engage in fasting or exercising excessively.

What causes bulimia nervosa in children?

Bulimia is not something that children choose. And it's not because of your parenting decisions that kids become bulimic.

Bulimia is caused by a child's brain's reaction to desires and messages about food, health, and body image. This is the result of a number of factors. Genetics, stress, and social and cultural demands to maintain a certain weight or appearance are among them.

Binge Eating Disorder

What is Binge Eating Disorder?

Binge eating disorder is an eating disorder that can affect children and teenagers. It involves the consumption of excessively large amounts of food in short periods. They usually do it in private and are embarrassed after doing so. Binge eating disorder affects children and teenagers who are unable to regulate their eating.

Binge eating disorder can affect children who are either normal weight or overweight. Children with binge eating disorder do not try to get rid of the food by vomiting or taking laxatives.

What causes binge eating disorder in children?

Binge eating disorder's exact cause is unknown. However, a number of factors are likely to be at play, including genetics, family eating habits, emotions, and eating habits such as skipping meals. Children will sometimes use food to comfort themselves or cope with negative emotions.

It's difficult to predict why children and teenagers may engage in binge eating, as they don't talk about or seek assistance for out-of-control eating because they feel guilty or embarrassed about it.

The Effects of Eating Disorders

Eating disorders can harm the child's body as well as their mind.

Body: Physical Effects of Eating Disorders

Eating disorders can cause a variety of physical effects, both minor and major. One may even experience physical symptoms that are more noticeable such as having brittle hair and nails, they might become extremely thin or lose muscle mass, and will often have dry skin. However, eating disorders can lead to other health problems, for example, Type II diabetes and pancreatitis. Eating disorders can also have long-term bodily consequences, such as:

- **Heart Problems.** Malnutrition or frequent vomiting can cause heart damage. A child's heartbeat might be slow, rapid, or irregular. He or she could potentially suffer from low blood pressure. When the body is deprived of calories, it will begin to break down its own muscles and tissue for energy. It can sometimes affect its most important muscle, the heart. Bulimia can lead to heart failure because vomiting depletes the body of essential

minerals and electrolytes such as potassium, which the heart needs to function.
- **Malnutrition and dehydration.** Restricting your diet or eliminating essential nutrients from your diet might result in significant deficits in your body. Dehydration occurs when your body does not receive enough fluids to function correctly, which can result in kidney failure, seizures, exhaustion, diarrhoea, or muscle cramps. Anorexia can cause dehydration, which might result in urine that is extremely concentrated. It's also possible that your child will produce more pee. When the kidneys' ability to concentrate urine is impeded, this can happen. When your child's weight returns to normal, kidney function usually returns to normal.

Malnutrition implies your body isn't getting enough nutrients and proteins, which can stifle your immune system and cause a variety of health issues, including anaemia. A low red blood cell count affects about one-third of anorexic children (mild anaemia). A low white blood cell count affects about half of the children who have this health concern (leukopenia).
- **Slowed Brain Function.** The brain weighs three pounds and uses up to one-fifth of the calories consumed by the rest of the body. Dieting, fasting, starving, and/or inconsistent eating, depletes the brain's ability to function and focus.
- **Gastroparesis.** This is also known as slowed digestion. The stomach is programmed to empty itself

and digest what you eat. So, when you vomit or starve yourself, it can affect how it works. This can result in:

1. Nausea and vomiting
2. Stomach pain and bloating
3. Blood sugar fluctuations
4. Blocked intestines from solid masses of undigested food
5. Bacterial infections
6. Eating small amounts make you full quickly

- **Hormone Levels Drop.** When we consume fat and cholesterol, our bodies use them to produce hormones. Sex hormones (meaning oestrogen and testosterone) levels can drop when we reduce the amount of fats and calories in our diets. Thyroid hormone levels may drop as well. These can cause a young woman's period to stop, but they can also have serious effects, such as bone loss. Teenagers with anorexia may also have lower levels of growth hormones. This could explain why some children with anorexia experience delayed growth.
- **Hypothermia.** With a consistent eating disorder, a child's body might find it difficult to regulate its temperatures. This means that the temperatures can drop significantly without notice or even reason. The body may become hypothermic if it does not have enough energy to fuel its metabolic fire.

- **Deterioration of the Oesophagus and Teeth.** Excessive vomiting from a purging eating disorder like bulimia can wear down the child's teeth enamel as well as their oesophagus, owing to the acidity. Purging eating disorders can cause rupture of the oesophagus.

Mind: Psychological Effects of Eating Disorders

The psychological effects of an eating disorder might be much more severe than the medical effects. Undereating, binge eating, and purging lowers self-confidence, self-esteem and happiness. Children with eating disorders often face one or more of the following issues:

- **Social Isolation.** Children with eating disorders struggle in silence. The child may distance themselves from their friends and family, be unwilling to share personal information with others, or be picky about what they eat. These tendencies are most likely a result of the shame and humiliation the children feel about their eating habits. The child may lack trust, and this maintains the isolation.
- **Loneliness.** The child may feel uncomfortable around others where there is food. Because of this, the child may shun social occasions such as family dinners, birthday celebrations, and family reunions. Food brings people together in every culture, and a child with an

eating disorder is uncomfortable around food in the presence of others. Avoiding social gatherings where food is being served might result in extreme loneliness, self-doubt, and depression.
- **Depression.** Eating disorders have a significant impact on the child's mood. Undernourishment in the body causes changes in the brain, which typically result in a negative shift in mood, which leads to depression in children suffering from anorexia.
- **Suicidal Ideation.** Eating disorders can be debilitating illnesses, especially for children as they are still developing. These disorders take away the child's health, happiness, and social life. They wreak havoc on the mind and the body, and children may grow tired of these feelings of hopelessness and end up taking their lives.

Who Children should Talk to when Experiencing Eating Disorders

When it comes to eating disorders, children become socially withdrawn and develop trust issues, even with their parents, as they feel ashamed of themselves. Or they may believe that telling anyone will result in them being humiliated by the person. Some children may even become touchy, or grumpy and refuse to acknowledge that they have a problem.

There are always signs of eating disorders, so as a parent, guardian, teacher or a close family friend, when you notice these signs, it is up to you to take action by talking to them. If they do not come to you, go to them. Continuing to talk about their situation is necessary for their healing. It may be tough for them to express their emotions, so be patient and pay attention to what they're trying to communicate.

If you sense that your child may have an eating disorder, seek help from health care professionals such as your child's paediatrician, as they can help identify early onset of an eating disorder and help prevent it from developing.

Professionals

The first line of defence can be the child's primary care physician. Then look into therapists or eating disorder programs as options. A trusted counsellor, a family doctor, a psychologist, a psychiatrist, or a social worker. Any professional that the parent speaks with should have experience with eating disorders.

Family Members

Parents are urged to speak with one another and devise a plan for assigning responsibility for each meal and snack.

Educators

School instructors, guidance counsellors, and the school principal can be extremely helpful.

Peers

Support groups are great.

How can Eating Disorders Affect their Adult Lives Later?
Eating disorders in childhood and adolescence are associated with an increased risk of developing a variety of physical and mental health issues in early adulthood.

It is harder for your body to recover from the severe effects of an eating disorder as you get older, making them even more harmful for adults. If anorexia is not treated in adolescence, for example, when the child becomes an adult, she is more likely to have a miscarriage, a caesarean delivery, and a baby with low birth weight or birth defects.

Children and adolescents who have been chronically ill with the disorder for many years, taking them into adulthood, may experience other physical health effects such as:

1. increased risk of high blood pressure
2. kidney failure
3. anaemia
4. heart disease
5. cognitive problems

In adulthood, they are at a significant risk for mental problems such as anxiety and depression. Eating disorders put a person under a lot of stress since they involve rapid weight loss and starving themself, which increases the possibilities of anxiety.

They may develop depression as a co-occurring illness. With someone suffering from anorexia, being malnourished and extremely underweight can create chemical changes in the brain. These changes may have a negative effect on mood, potentially leading to depression.

Stories about Eating Disorders
Anorexia Nervosa

Jessica is 16 years old and lives at home with her parents and younger brother. She has maintained a healthy weight throughout her teenage years, but she is self-conscious about her body weight and form. She frequently compares her weight to that of other girls and women she's met or seen on tv or on magazine covers. She then views herself as being overweight.

She often looks in the mirror, checking her body weight. At about 14 years old, she noticed that her thighs were touching and started dieting, at first just on and off, but then she started dieting regularly. She chose to become a vegetarian at the age of 15 and began eliminating various foods from her diet. At this age, she was 5'8" and 115 pounds, but dropped to 95 pounds by her 16th birthday.

Instead of feeling relieved by her weight loss, she continues to regard herself as overweight. Throughout the day, she weighs herself. She spends the majority of her time obsessing over her weight. Other activities she used to enjoy, such as schoolwork and going out with her friends, are replaced with her obsession with her weight. She feels alone and she also continues to lose weight.

Bulimia Nervosa

Lacy's history with eating disorder began when she was just 13 years old. Lacy was in middle school and was a cheerleader. She was always thinner than her classmates. However, in the eighth grade, Lacy began to get taller and started gaining weight. She had a hard time dealing with these changes, especially given that she was a cheerleader.

She began to restrict her food intake. She would skip breakfast and eat only a small portion at lunch. All day long, her stomach would growl, but she still wouldn't eat. She'd be starving by the time she got home from cheer practice in the afternoon.

She would eat whatever she could get her hands on—cookies, candies, potato chips, and a variety of other junk food. She'd binge and get this sudden rush from eating all that food. After binging, she would purge. She would feel lighter afterwards.

How to Deal with Eating Disorders

When it comes to managing eating disorders in young children, there are numerous factors to consider. Regaining weight is critical for the child's physical and nutritional well-being to be restored. Because parents and caregivers play such an important role in the lives of their children, family-based intervention and treatment are frequently advised.

Parents frequently blame themselves for their child's eating disorder, therefore, when parents gain confidence and empowerment in their ability to help their child, the outcome is frequently better.

Become a member of an eating disorder support group. Parents might benefit from eating disorder support groups in a variety of ways. To begin with, knowing that you are not alone in having a child with food-related challenges might be reassuring. Second, you'll get helpful hints from other parents on how to help your child manage their disorder. Finally, you have a safe place to express your accomplishments, frustrations, and experiences.

A support group can be a useful resource whether you want to learn more about your child eating disorder or simply learn how to communicate to a teenager about an eating disorder.

Become knowledgeable about eating problems. Learning about eating disorders will enable you to be a more supporting factor in your child's managing of the disorder. There are a variety of resources available to help you learn more about eating disorders, including the following:

1. Research adolescent eating problems by reading books, journal articles, and research.

2. On your drive to work or scheduled activities, listen to podcasts about adolescent eating problems.

3. Consult a qualified dietician to learn how to prepare therapeutic meals and choose foods.

Make a promise to yourself to spend more time with your child. More time spent with your child is a wonderful way to demonstrate your love and support. Selecting shared activities that both you and your child can enjoy is a good place to start. Avoid food-related activities and events as much as possible, especially while your child is undergoing therapy. You can gradually begin to reintroduce food-related events once your child has finished treatment.

How can Children Heal from Eating Disorders?

It's natural for the parent or guardian to feel overwhelmed when their child is diagnosed with an eating disorder. Many parents are unsure how to cope with their teen's eating issue, and it's typical for them to feel helpless. The good news is that they can play an important role in helping children dealing with their eating disorders and perhaps assist them to avoid relapsing.

Have patience. Patience is the first step toward successful recovery from an eating disorder. It is possible to make a long-term recovery, but the treatment procedure requires time and cannot be rushed. The therapy procedure might last anywhere from a few weeks to more than a month, depending on the severity of your child's eating disorder. It may take years of therapy and treatment to fully recover from a major or persistent eating disorder.

Tell the child you love them. Your unconditional love can make a significant difference in your child's healing. When it comes to expressing your love and support, the most important thing to keep in mind is the importance of timing. When your child hits a treatment milestone, it is usually simpler to demonstrate your support. However, setbacks can occur both during and after treatment. When your child is going through a difficult period, he or she needs your love and support the most.

Go to your child's appointments with them. Three goals are achieved by driving your child to partial treatment or outpatient therapy visits. First and foremost, the parents are sure that their child is adhering to their treatment plan. Second, the parent show that they support their treatment efforts.

Monitor your child's overall health. Bulimia and anorexia put children and teenagers at risk for a multitude of physical health problems. Children and teenagers with anorexia, for example, are more likely to experience constipation, menstrual abnormalities, and arrhythmia. Tooth damage, electrolyte imbalances, and heart failure are among concerns related with bulimia. If you observe any of these symptoms, contact your child's paediatrician or primary care physician at once.

EATING DISORDERS HELP
1- **NATIONAL EATING DISORDERS HELPLINE (US)**
CALL: 1-800-931-2237
EMAIL: info@NationalEatingDisorders.org

2- **CHILDLINE (UK)**
CALL: 0800 1111
CHAT: 121 counsellor chat

Child Abuse

There is a wider number of children experiencing child abuse and this may look different for each child/family. In my professional life as a teacher, one of the challenges I often face is parents not understanding what child abuse is and when they themselves are abusing their child/ren.

In this chapter, we will explore this topic. My hope is that, as a parent, you will understand any abusive behaviour you are exhibiting and commit to changing that behaviour. As someone who may know of a child experiencing any form of child abuse, try to get them and/or their family the help they need. Do not turn a blind eye to child abuse.

What is Child Abuse?

Child abuse is defined as any act or failure to act by a parent or guardian that causes a child's death, major physical or emotional pain, sexual abuse, or exploitation. It is any act or failure to act that poses a serious risk of serious injury to a child.

Physical abuse, mental abuse, sexual abuse, and neglect are all forms of child abuse.

Physical Abuse

Physical abuse is defined as any act or failure to act that causes a child to suffer non-accidental physical harm or puts the child's physical well-being in danger. Hitting, burning, choking, kicking, punching, restraint, and the use of a weapon are all examples.

Children who are being physically abused will have unexplained bruises that include fractures or scrapes. They will have nervous, hyperactive, aggressive, disruptive and destructive behaviours, unwarranted fear of a parent or guardian, anxiety and an unusual aversion to physical contact.

Emotional Abuse

Emotional abuse is when a child is subjected to words, attitudes, or behaviours that cause substantial emotional or psychological harm. It includes exposing children to activities or situations that may cause emotional harm, such as negative criticism, insults, or any other type of vilification.

Children being emotionally abused may have delayed physical or emotional development, very poor self-esteem, depression and/or suicide thoughts or attempts, speech disorders, antisocial or destructive behaviour, and delinquent behaviour, particularly among teenagers.

Sexual Abuse

Sexual abuse is the action of engaging or luring a child to participate in any type of sexual activity, with or without the kid's knowledge or agreement. It can include genital fondling, oral sex, and vaginal or anal penetration with a finger, penis, or other object.

Sexual abuse includes exhibitionism (public display of the private parts), allowing minors to view or participate in the production of pornographic material, and sexually provocative behaviour directed at a child.

Children being sexually abused tend to have a thorough and sophisticated understanding of sexual behaviours. They also engage in sexual activities inappropriate for a child's age and may experience sleep disturbances/nightmares.

Neglect

When the care, discipline, and/or supervision of a child is disregarded to a great extent, the child is being neglected. Neglect encompasses a caregiver's inability to meet a child's basic needs, abandonment, and putting a child in danger. This form of abuse can be physical, psychological/emotional, or educational. Neglected children's medical needs have gone unmet, there is consistent absenteeism from school, they beg or steal, experience consistent hunger, have unsuitable clothing and poor hygiene, and has a pale or listless look.

Physical neglect involves failing to provide adequate food and clothing, as well as proper medical attention, supervision, and weather protection (heat or cold).

Abandonment by a parent is also a form of physical neglect.

Failure to offer proper schooling or special educational requirements, permitting numerous truancies, or failing to register or enrol the child in school are all examples of educational neglect.

Child Labour

The term "child labour" is defined by the International Labour Organization (ILO) as "work that deprives children of their youth, their potential, and their dignity, and that is damaging to their physical and mental development." Examples of child labour include the employment of children in a night club or bar, having a child participate in indecent and immoral acts such as exotic dance and pornography; and knowingly renting or allowing the use of one's property for these activities, putting a child to work in any sort of night job or industrial enterprise that is likely to be hazardous, interfere with the child's education, or be injurious to the child's health or physical, mental, spiritual, or social development.

What are the Causes of Child Abuse?
Domestic Violence

Children who grow up in homes where domestic violence is common are more likely to become victims of abuse themselves. Men who abuse their wives also tend to turn that abuse onto their children.

Alcohol and Drug Abuse

Child abuse can be caused by parents who have a history of alcohol and drug abuse. Substance abuse is one of the leading causes of child abuse and mistreatment, which includes physical abuse and purposeful neglect. Children under the age of five are more likely to be abused by a parent who abuses alcohol or drugs.

Untreated Mental Illness

Child abuse is frequently caused by a parent's untreated mental illness. Manic depression or any other mental disorder can lead to the parent's inability to care for their children. A mother may withdraw from her children or, in the worst-case scenario, feel that the child is plotting against her and harm the child. Abuse of a child is frequently the result of a parent's grief.

Lack of Parenting Skills

While most parents are naturally good at caring for their children, a select few may be unable to properly cater to their physical and emotional needs. Many parents mistakenly believe that disciplining their children is the same as abusing them, and they will require counselling to better understand their responsibilities as parents.

Stress and Lack of Support

When their parents or guardians are stressed, many children are subjected to psychological abuse. It's challenging for parents to deal with a child's emotional demands, especially when they're in a stressful circumstance. Divorce, relationship problems, financial concerns, and job-related issues can all lead to parents abusing their children.

The Effects of Child Abuse

Child abuse can have significant effects on all aspects of a child's self-esteem, development, and their ability to function. Adverse effects are generally related to all forms of abuse. When the abuse is repetitive, which it usually is, it can have long term effects on children, affecting their mental, emotional, physical health, and more aspects of their lives.

Psychological Effects

Attachment and Interpersonal Relationship Problems

Abused and neglected babies and young infants are more likely to have insecure or disorganized attachment problems with their primary caregiver. Attachment patterns between a child and his or her caregiver are critical for a child's early emotional and social development. The parent/caregiver, who should be the primary provider of safety, protection, and comfort for children with insecure attachments, becomes a source of danger or injury.

Babies and infants who do not have the stability and support of a primary caregiver may find it difficult to trust others when they are distressed, which can lead to anxiety or anger.

Children's normal developmental processes are disrupted by insecure attachments, which can have a significant impact on a child's capacity to communicate and connect with others, as well as create healthy relationships, throughout their lives. Child abuse has been linked to dysfunctional peer relationships in childhood and adolescence. Furthermore, problems in peer relationships may be a precursor to problems in love relationships.

Learning and Developmental Problems

There is a strong association between child abuse and learning difficulties and poor academic performance. Abuse in the early years of life can have a significant impact on an infant's development, particularly in the important areas of speech and language.

Mental Health

Child abuse can affect a child's mental health for the rest of his or her life. Post-traumatic stress disorder (PTSD), attention deficit hyperactivity disorder (ADHD), anxiety, and mood disorders (depression) are all common among adolescents and adults who were abused as children.

Youth Suicide

According to research, child abuse increases the risk of teenagers having suicidal thoughts and attempting suicide. Because they are unable to take the pain anymore, they think that ending their life is the best way out, as it will relieve them of their suffering.

Behavioural Effects

Child abuse can cause behavioural problems in children and teenagers. The following are some examples of how child abuse can affect behaviour:

Harmful Sexual Habits. According to research, abused or neglected children are more likely to engage in sexual risk-taking as they enter adolescence, including having more sexual partners, initiating sexual behaviour earlier, and engaging in transactional sex, all of which increase their risk of contracting a sexually transmitted disease.

Juvenile Delinquency. Children who are subjected to physical and emotional abuse are more likely to develop antisocial behaviours and build ties with other antisocial people, according to research. Furthermore, there is a distinction between how child abuse affects delinquent behaviour in girls and boys. In general, girls display behaviours that are internalised (e.g., anxiety, withdrawing from social and even important activities, depression/sadness). Boys on the other hand, will display external behaviours (e.g., becoming bullies, being violent, joining gangs). This does not mean that one gender cannot react in each of these ways.

Aggression. A child's reaction to stress is often a display of anger and emotional expression. Children experience distress and frustration as a result of the stress that comes with any type of abuse. Excessive rage manifests itself in aggressive behaviour and fights with caregivers and peers. When someone is physically abused, this type of reaction is amplified.

Physical Effects

The biology of the body develops from birth through adolescence. The environment influences biological function in some ways. The immune system and the body's stress response system may not develop normally if a child grows up fearful or under continuous or extremely stressful situations which is the case when they are being abused. When the child is later subjected to even moderate amounts of stress, these systems may react as though the person is under extreme stress. For example, they may exhibit strong physiological reactions, such as breathing rapidly or their heart pounding.

The development of the brain and the nervous system may be hindered by the stress that comes from an abusive environment. In neglectful situations, for example, a lack of mental stimulation may prevent the brain from reaching its full potential. Chronic or recurrent physical symptoms, such as migraine or abdominal pain, may develop in children experiencing child abuse.

Children who are abused may experience body dysregulation, which means they over-respond or under-respond to sensory stimuli. They can be oversensitive to light, sounds, scents, or touch. They can also suffer from anaesthesia and analgesia, where they are oblivious to pain, tough, or internal bodily sensations. Thus, they may harm themselves without noticing or complain about persistent discomfort in numerous areas of the body without any physical cause.

Who Children should Talk to when Experiencing Child Abuse

Children who are being abused should tell a responsible adult. Who? Someone at school, such as a school counsellor, nurse, teacher, or coach, could be informed. Alternatively, they can inform a friend's mother or father, big brother or big sister. This can be done in person or over the phone, or in writing via a note, email, or letter. This can be difficult since a child may have been scared into remaining silent. However, it is critical for children to continue to report abuse until an adult intervenes and the violence ceases.

They can tell someone on the phone or by text at a hotline service if they don't have a trusted adult to turn to:

1. If the child is in the United States or Canada, they should call 1-800-4-A-CHILD. People are available to assist children who have been harmed at any time of the day or night.

2. They should call 911 if they are in danger, making sure to include details such as their first name and address so that they can be assisted.

If the child suspects someone else is being mistreated, they can help by informing a parent or another adult, such as a teacher or their own parents.

How can Child Abuse Affect their Adult Lives Later?
The effects of child abuse can linger for a long time in the minds of survivors. Adults who have buried their past of child abuse may continue to suffer from PTSD, eating disorders, substance addiction, depression, anxiety, low self-esteem, rage, guilt, learning difficulties, physical disease, unsettling memories, and dissociation, among

other things. The difficulty of creating and maintaining adult relationships is one such issue.

Child abuse can have a negative impact on a survivor's personality development and capacity to regulate their emotions, leading to self-destructive and impulsive behaviour such as repeated self-harm or suicide attempts in adulthood. Children who have been abused repeatedly over time may undergo dissociation and enter trance-like states in which they relive abusive experiences in their adult lives, which are often triggered by reminders of the abuse.

Although the majority of child abuse survivors do not go on to abuse or neglect their own children, some evidence suggests that adults who were abused or neglected as children are more likely to engage in intergenerational abuse or neglect than adults who were not abused as children. Growing up in an abusive family setting can teach children that using violence and aggressiveness as a means of resolving interpersonal conflict is a valid option, increasing the risk that the cycle of violence will continue when they reach adulthood.

Adults who were abused as children, particularly women, are at danger of being abused again later in life, according to research. All types of childhood victimization (physical abuse, sexual abuse, and neglect) are linked to a higher risk of re-victimization later in life. Child abuse is linked to an increased chance of physical and sexual assault/abuse, kidnapping/stalking, and having a family member murdered or commit suicide, according to the findings.

Women who have experienced physical child abuse or observed parental violence may be more vulnerable to adult victimization because they are more likely to have low self-esteem and may have learned that violence is a typical response to conflict.

Stories about Child Abuse
Physical Abuse

Terry is the middle child of three children. Her mother was abused by her father for years, and the kids would often be present during this abuse. Terry's mother managed to escape her father one night, but she left them behind. Terry's father started abusing the children after she left. He would hit them and throw anything he could find at them. Terry's older sister was subjected to heavy lashings whenever dinner wasn't ready on time, which was frequently because she had to be taking care of her and their younger brother.

Emotional Abuse

Emma is 16 years old, and her school is having a spring formal. She is very excited, as she had never been to one of the school dances before. Her crush, Damien, asks her to the dance and Emma happily accepts. Emma spends most of last period thinking about what she is going to wear and how much fun she is going to have. When school ends, she rushes to her mom's waiting car. She gets in and starts excitedly telling her mom about the dance and Damien. Her mother looks at her and laughs. She asks her how many times she has told her that nobody will like someone like her. Her mother starts making fun of her hair and her clothes like she always does. She calls her ugly and too short. Her mother tells her to stop thinking about the dance because someone like her would never be expected to go anyways. Emma starts crying, feeling humiliated and hurt from her mother's constant berating. Her mother tells her to wipe her tears and then drives off.

Sexual Abuse

Steven, at nine years old, was sexually abused by his neighbour. Steven belonged to a single-parent household, so most of the time his mother was out working, trying to make ends meet. Steven would stay with his neighbour across the street until his mother came and got him. He was in the living room with his neighbour one evening when she began to excessively touch and fondle him. Steven knew this was wrong but thought that if he spoke up, his neighbour would make him stay outside. This continued for weeks, until his neighbour went further and forced him to have intercourse with her. Steven began to feel very angry with his mother for what was happening to him, thinking that if she wasn't working he would not be subjected to abuse.

Neglect

Ms Taylor, a second grade teacher noticed that one of her students, Malik, was almost always feeling ill or tired and sleeping in class. His clothes had stains and tears on them, and his hair was always dishevelled. Whenever she approached him, she noticed that he smelled, and he looked slightly underweight. Ms. Taylor suspected that Malik wasn't getting the care that he needed and was being neglected at home. She promised herself she would report it to the principal. Days past and Malik was still the same even after she spoke with the principal. One day when school ended, Ms. Taylor stayed back to do a little cleaning up. When she was about to leave the school, it was after 4 p.m. and she noticed that Malik was still sitting outside on a bench. She offered to drive him home. When they arrived, she told Malik she would like to speak with his parents. When she entered the house, the place was a mess and Malik's mother was asleep on the couch, surrounded by beer bottles.

How to Deal with Child Abuse

Child abuse is a common diagnosis in the United States, and it should be examined any time there is a risk of neglect, emotional, physical, or sexual abuse. Despite the fact that home visitation programs have proven to be helpful in avoiding child maltreatment, much of the approach to and management of child abuse is influenced by expert opinion or legal mandate. Child Protective Services must be notified if there is any suspicion of abuse. To properly diagnose and treat child abuse victims, a multidisciplinary approach is suggested; nonetheless, it is typically the responsibility of the family physician to recognize and treat these cases at the outset in order to avoid major morbidity and mortality.

Expectations. Parents can appreciate these children's bravery and strength by setting high standards for them. Because emotionality can obstruct thinking, it's critical to set fair goals and offer the necessary support for the child to feel secure in his or her ability. School can help children reclaim their self-confidence, establish themselves, and regard themselves as successful.

Structure. Children who have been abused may feel unable to control much of their surroundings. They may cope by: (a) refusing to try to control what happens around them; (b) attempting to manipulate everything they can by bossing peers and controlling belongings; and (c) expressing exaggerated feelings whenever they feel threatened. When these kids go off the handle for no apparent reason, it's possible that they're trying to gain control. Parents, guardians, teachers, any adult, should provide accurate information and create trust in order to let the child feel in charge in a positive way. Allowing children to express feelings through art, music, theatre, and/or creative writing when appropriate will also help them feel less constrained by pent-up emotion.

Identity. Children who have been abused in ways that met the needs of an adult while ignoring the needs of the child have a weak sense of personal identity. Parents and other adults can help by highlighting the child's abilities, for example, telling them, "You are a hard worker." Teachers can also assist abused children in developing a sense of personal identity by asking open-ended questions, administering interest inventories, and teaching decision-making and problem-solving skills. This will help to improve both their personal and social relationships.

Self-esteem. Children who have been abused have low self-esteem. By cultivating an environment that values each child's uniqueness, adults may help kids learn that they are respected, accepted, and capable. Children will learn to regard themselves as having something to contribute that others value. The child's sense of competence will be cultivated with each successful completion of a task.

Sense of belonging. Abused children believe they have done something wrong and are bad. They feel there is a reason for them to be isolated from others since they have hidden a secret from everyone. Teachers can provide designated spaces for possessions, showcase work in the classroom, and make a special effort to include these children in school activities to help them feel more at home. Support will also help abused children practice interacting in a nonthreatening environment by teaching social skills individually, in small groups, and through cooperative learning.

Social skills. Because abused children have not learnt to listen to their inner self, they may place a greater emphasis on satisfying and meeting the needs of others while ignoring their own. The child may have learned inappropriate behaviours and language as a result of being exposed to the adult world through an abusive relationship. The child may feel unworthy to interact with others on an equal footing and may be afraid of rejection. An environment that promotes kindness, acceptance of differences, clear rules and boundaries, and praise for little achievements will nurture a child who has been overlooked at home.

How can Children Heal from Child Abuse?
Growing up in a loving and caring home is essential for a child's development. These vulnerable abused and neglected children when given a loving and caring environment, a caregiver, and the right tools to heal, can not only heal, but thrive.

Build a Strong Bond with the Abused Child

Creating a safe emotional link with an abused child is one of the most crucial things a parent or caregiver can do. A strong adult attachment supports recovery through fostering a child's physical, social, and emotional growth. A child's trust, ability to form meaningful relationships, beneficial habits, and healing journey are all aided by a loving and safe attachment. Ensure that the child is protected and that previous experiences will not be repeated throughout the bonding phase.

Be present in the moment. Offer affection and support to the child on a regular basis to help them develop feelings of trust and safety.

Be reassuring. When the child is upset or acting out, provide emotional and loving support. This is an important moment to model good behaviours and provide appropriate shows of compassion and love to help the child regain his or her self-esteem.

Respect each other. Let the child know that you will respect their boundaries, physical or otherwise but you will also keep them safe.

Rebuild Resiliency and Cultivate a Safe Environment

Be patient and mindful. All children react to trauma in different ways; be patient with the child's reaction and stay present.

Be dependable and consistent. Regaining trust is one of the most challenging aspects of healing children. Keep your word and stick to it.

Show your support and affection. Your love and support can be communicated in a variety of ways, including words, hugs, and encouraging letters.

It takes a village. Family and friends play a critical role in a child's recovery and ability to re-establish trust in adults and others.

Allow the child to grieve and feel. Allow and encourage the child to express his or her emotions, which may include grief. Applaud their capacity to express themselves without resorting to bad behaviour.

Model/teach good habits. Make sure to teach and model appropriate emotional responses. Include healthy diet and exercise discussions.

CHILD ABUSE HELP
1- **Child Help USA 1.800.4 A Child**
   Call: 1-800-422-4453

Low Self-Esteem

There is so much in the world for our children to compare themselves to. Social media has opened up the world so much so that our children no longer have the pressures of the communities they live in but the entire world.

Like many adults, their self-esteem is often affected by what they see online as it seeps into how they perceive themselves and the world around them. This chapter takes a look at self-esteem and the challenges that our children and teens face in this regard.

What is Self-Esteem?

Self-esteem is one's perception of themself. Usually people have either high or low self-esteem and this can change depending on the situations and environments they find themselves in at a given time. Those who have high self-esteem and usually proud of themselves. They value their accomplishments. They are usually in control of their life and accept themselves as they are. They feel that they can trust themselves. These individuals think of themselves in a positive way. Although they have weaknesses, they also know that they have strengths and do not focus on the negatives to bring themselves down.

On the other hand, low self-esteem might make you feel full of self-doubt, be passive or submissive, or have difficulty trusting others. People with low self-esteem usually find it hard to take on criticism. They often feel that they are not loved and may even feel inferior to others. They can experience feeling confidence, but this is usually situation based. What this means is that they feel confident when they are good at something, like drawing, but inferior when they are in a space where they do not understand something.

No matter who you are, there will always be instances where you feel less confident. However, for people with a low self-esteem, they feel less confident most of the times. Being dissatisfied with themselves happens often. Luckily, by understanding/accepting that you have a low self-esteem and making the decision to practise improving it, you can improve your self-esteem.

It is important to note that your abilities or lack thereof, doesn't really affect your self-esteem. What does is your perception, how you actually see yourself in your own mind. No matter how good you are at something, even if everyone praises you for it, if you do not think that you are good enough, you will not be confident about doing it.

Also important is the fact that your self-esteem can change as is usually affected by different things happening in your life. For example, you might begin to have a low self-esteem at school if you are being bullied online. Your perception of how you are viewed by everyone will change because of what the bully is saying about you, although your friends at school do not agree with what is being said.

What are the Causes of Low Self-Esteem?

Self-esteem in young children is usually rather high, but as the teen years approach, low self-esteem may become more of a problem. Low self-esteem first appears throughout pre-adolescence for a variety of interconnected factors:

Lack of Parental Support

When a child's parents does not pay enough attention to them, it is difficult for the child to feel driven to want more and take on new endeavours. It makes the child feel unimportant, unwanted, and forgotten. It also makes the child feel as if none of their accomplishments are significant.

Comparing themselves to Others

Children begin to actively compare themselves to their peers between the ages of six and eleven. This social comparison are a result of cognitive and social reasons.

Self-comparison, according to psychologist Erik Erikson, sets the foundation for the most difficult struggle that children of this age encounter. He believed their main issue is about creating a sense of industry, or skill, while avoiding a sense of inferiority.

Feelings of Incompetency

Some children, as Erikson pointed out, come to a realization that their efforts aren't as good as their peers' and begin to have feelings of inferiority. It's worth noting, though, that feeling incompetent does not always equate to low self-esteem. If a child does not care much about something and underperform, their self-esteem is likely to not be affected. If, on the other hand, he is inept in an area that he values, such as academics, he is at risk of developing low self-esteem.

Performance Pressure

During the tween years, there is also an increase in performance pressure. During early and middle childhood, parents and teachers are more likely to praise any effort, no matter how small or insignificant, good or bad. Adults begin to expect more from children as they approach adolescence; effort is still important, but performance is even more so. As a result, tweens not only create comparisons between themselves and their friends, but they also see adults do so.

Perceived Disapproval from Others

As the expectations of parents and teachers rise, tweens start to perceive their disapproval. The child's self-esteem being affected is dependent upon the adult(s) disapproval of the child's attempts. If the criticism comes from someone the child dislikes, such as an untrustworthy teacher, the child is unlikely to take the criticism seriously, and his or her self-esteem will remain high. Low self-esteem might develop if a child perceives that a beloved parent or trusted coach has let them down. As a result, it's apparent that parents may play an important role in assisting children in maintaining healthy self-esteem.

The Effects of Low Self-esteem

Self-esteem is a reflection of how your child feels about themself and influences how they approach the world. Although a child's self-esteem changes slightly from day to day, they have a basic sense of their worth and value. Their actions, body language, behaviour, and entire demeanour will reflect their low self-esteem.

Avoidance Behaviours

If a child has poor self-esteem, she or he will be hesitant to interact with new people or situations. If this is the case, they may feel awkward and shy away from new situations. They will often be afraid to take risks or leave their comfort zone. The child may miss out on key social opportunities and settings where they could learn and grow from a new experience if they continue to behave in this way.

The child might criticize themself and their abilities. He or she may be unduly critical of their abilities or their appearance. They most likely speak negatively about the world in general. Their body language, for example, slumped shoulders, sad expression on their faces, and downcast eyes will reveal a lack of confidence even if they don't say anything

Lack of Effort

A child who has low self-esteem may believe they are incompetent or unqualified to complete tasks. They may give up and walk away if they try a new activity and fails at it. A child with a stronger self-esteem is more likely to try again even if they failed at the first attempt.

Emotional Toll

When a child has poor self-esteem, he or she may experience a variety of negative emotions.

Who Children Should Talk to When Experiencing Low Self-Esteem

If a parent is worried that their child has low self-esteem and it is affecting their daily life, or their development, seeking professional help is crucial. Speaking to the child's paediatrician, the child's school, and even a counsellor are good places to start.

Children can talk with a peer buddy or a mentor. Being more a part of the school community can help them talk about it, for example joining a club.

How can Low Self-esteem Affect their Adult Lives Later?

Low self-esteem can have an impact on a child's thoughts, feelings, and behaviour patterns. You'll find that children who had low self-esteem growing up, and never rectified those feelings, when they are adults will criticize themselves. Some may even go out of their way to ensure that they remain in everyone's good graces, keeping everyone happy.

Low self-esteem in children can affect them in adulthood. How? Children who suffer from low self-esteem underestimate themselves and know nothing really of self-love and being self-responsible, when they grow up to be adults, they struggle to care for themselves.

They grow up believing, consciously or unconsciously, that they are undeserving of love and of having their needs addressed. It is due to a deeper psychological conviction that they are not important enough, that they are not deserving of it, that they can't have it, or that they don't matter.

Children with low self-esteem, because they are of the belief that they are undeserving, put their needs on the back burner and try to make others happy. As an adult, they find it difficult to ask for what they want because they do not want to give the impression that they are needy or cannot do something without help.

People with a low self-esteem experience a lot of self-doubt. They second-guess themselves a lot, which affects their ability to make decisions as well as how they progress in their lives. As adults, they have a hard time making decisions because they are afraid that they might be making the wrong one. When they do make a decision, they tend to worry and stress that they made the wrong choice. They distrust their own judgments and are more likely to listen to what others have to say rather than sticking to their decisions. For example, a son who calls his mother to get her opinion every time he is to make a decision regarding his business.

When a child grows up having low self-esteem, accepting positive feedback as an adult can be difficult. They find it difficult to take compliments from others since they do not have a favourable opinion of themselves.

Positive feedback is frequently greeted with scepticism and distrust because these complimenting statements contradict their self-perceptions. They may believe the other person is being sarcastic or even harsh. For example, their boss compliments them on a job well done but they believe their boss is making fun of them.

Because they lacked confidence in their abilities from they were children, as adults, they doubt their ability to accomplish anything, to be successful. They develop a fear of failing. While they may be afraid of failure, they tend to avoid challenges or give up without giving it their all.

Children who suffer from low self-esteem believe there is a slim chance that the future will be better. As adults, they find it difficult to engage in actions that would result in positive changes in their lives because of their feelings of hopelessness. They won't apply for that job because they won't get it. They won't apply for that promotion because there's no way their cubicle neighbour won't beat them out for it.

Stories about Low Self-Esteem
Scenario 1

Sarah is in high school, is 5'9 and weighs 200 pounds. Because of this, she is very shy and quiet. She always keeps a low profile at school, afraid that others would comment on her appearance. She always walks through the halls with her head held down and never speaks up in class. Sarah has a crush on one of her classmates and told her friend. When her classmate finds out, he laughs at her and calls her disgusting. Sarah is embarrassed and can't wait to get home and lock herself away in her room. After this experience, she begins to believe that she is disgusting, and no one will ever want to be with her. She looks at herself in the mirror with disdain and constantly berates herself.

Scenario 2

Josh is twelve years old and lives with his mom, dad, and older sister. His mother is a doctor, and his father owns his own company. His sister is in her final year of college and always gets good grades. Josh isn't doing well in school and often gets Cs and Ds. His teachers constantly call him stupid and tell him he's going nowhere. At home, he receives the same negative feedback from his family. His sister tells him he's dumb and his mother and father laughs at him. Josh finds himself starting to believe them, and self-criticizes himself. He never stands up to his family or his teachers.

How to Deal with Low Self-Esteem

Children learn and grow when they try new things, confront problems, and recover. Hence, self-esteem is important in their growth.

Children's self-esteem is built on the foundation of warm and loving connections that make them feel valued and worthy. A child's relationships are formed on a foundation of responsive, loving interactions. Family rituals are also significant because they strengthen family bonds and provide a sense of belonging for the child.

So how can a child deal with low self-esteem? It starts with the child's parents/guardians.

Parents should give their children with low self-esteem a balanced feedback. This is about applauding the child for trying something new, doing their best, or giving it their all. For example, they can be told, "Well done for running for class monitor and giving it your all. I am proud of you."

Adults who children look up to should help them deal with low self-esteem by emphasizing that loss is an inevitable aspect of life. Avoid asking the child, "Did you win?" Instead, ask the child, "Did you have fun?" This demonstrates to your child that you value them regardless of whether they win or lose, and encourages them to do so as well.

Family meals can be a simple yet effective approach for children of all ages to improve their sense of worth and belonging. Because children can all help with a family meal, such as setting the table, cleaning vegetables, tossing a salad, and so on. Family meals can also provide an opportunity for everyone to discuss topics that are important to them.

If things don't go as planned the first time, encourage the child to try again. For example, saying, "Go on, how about you give it another shot. I believe you can do it." This will help the child to become more resilient.

How can Children Heal from Low Self-Esteem?

Children can heal from low self-esteem. It may take some time but with help, they can certainly overcome this struggle. Children can make a list of the skills they have with the help of their parents or guardians. Can the child draw or sing? Are they an excellent reader? Do they excel in a sport? Are they really good at telling jokes?

Have children practice what they're good at. Parents, teacher, guardians can help them to think of ways they can accomplish some of the things they're strong in on a daily basis.

Try saying "I can!" instead of "I can't." Children should rid themselves of sayings things such as, "I'm not good at this" or "I can't do it?" "It's too difficult for me." That's them being critical of themself. Help them to make the decision to change their viewpoint. Reinforce positive statements such as "I can do this," or "I can handle this," and "I'll do my best." They also shouldn't be afraid to ask for help when they need it.

When they give it their all, they will feel good about themselves. Their self-esteem will increase when they work hard.

Spending time with the individuals they care about, participating in activities that they enjoy with their parents, friends, and family, will give them that sense of belonging. And this boosts one's self-esteem.

Child counselling can also help increase their self-esteem if they need more help.

LOW SELF-ESTEEM HELP
1- **KIDS HELP PHONE (USA)**
   Call 1-800-668-6868
   Text 686868

2- **KIDS INSPIRE (UK)**
   Call 01245 348707

Social Pressure

In the previous chapter, I mentioned how the world has opened up to our children and how it affects their self-esteem. Well, it is not only their self-esteem that is affected. Their entire lives are affected at times.

There is a lot of social pressure that our kids are experiencing today, from their peers at school to other children half-way across the globe. They want to fit in, to be liked, to be with the in-crowd. For some children, the need to fit in can have a negative impact on their lives.

This chapter of the book takes a look at social pressures in the lives of our teens and children.

What is Social Pressure?

Social pressure is the act of another person or group exerting influence over a person or group. Social pressure, like group pressure, consists of rational argument and persuasion (informational influence), conformity (normative influence), and direct forms of influence, such as demands, threats, or personal attacks on one side, and offers of rewards or social acceptability on the other (interpersonal influence).

When a child is growing up, they experience social pressure, and parents should always be prepared to deal with it. It is difficult for a child to cope throughout childhood when others try to influence how they act and do things. It's critical to teach your young children how to choose their friends wisely and how to say no politely without jeopardizing their friendships.

Peer pressure and academic demands are examples of social pressures that children may encounter in their daily lives.

Peer Pressure

Human beings need people in different ways and so do children and teenagers. Their social and emotional development is dependent on the friendships they create as they grow. Their influence begins at a young age and grows throughout adolescence. As children grow and mature, it is natural, healthy, and vital for them to have and rely on friends. Peers can be helpful and encouraging. They can assist one another in learning new skills or pique each other's interest in books, music, or extracurricular activities. Peers, however, can sometimes have a negative influence on one another. For example, a group of kids at school may try to persuade another child to skip class with them, a friend on the child's basketball team may persuade them to be cruel to another player and never pass the ball to him, or a child in their neighbourhood may persuade them to shoplift with her.

Academic Pressure

Academic pressure is where a child is burdened by time and energy demands in order to meet certain academic goals that are either set by their parents, family members, teachers, themselves, or society. It can be a positive force that motivates children to do well or a negative force that causes children to experience anxiety when studying.

The Causes of Children Giving in to Social Pressure

Growing up, children are exposed to peer pressure from both inside and beyond the family: friend groups, classmates, teams, and even older siblings. But what causes children to yield to the demands of peer pressure. Adopting some of the attitudes and behaviours of their social group is usually highly significant to their sense of belonging and acceptance. The following are some causes of why children give in to peer pressure.

Weak Personality

Children are yet to develop a solid personality and peer pressure can be highly effective on them. The weaker the child's individuality is, the easier it is for others to persuade them to act in certain ways. Because character and personality need time to develop and grow, children and teenagers are more susceptible to peer pressure than older people with more life experience. As a result, the weaker a person's personality is, the more likely they are to be influenced by peer pressure.

The Fear of Rejection

Children, when growing up, are taught morals and values and they even form their own opinions and views about what is right and what is wrong, but because of this fear that they have of being rejected, they are hesitant to express their own opinions. If the fear of rejection is excessive, the child may give up all of their beliefs and views in order to conform to the attitudes and value systems of a group. Fear of rejection is a powerful motivator for pack behaviour and peer pressure.

Social Acceptance

Children, especially teenagers, crave social acceptance. They want to fit in, to feel like they belong somewhere. Fitting in, on the other hand, necessitates the abandonment of many of one's own views and characteristics. Children who are yearning to fit in are easy candidates for peer pressure, and certain groups of children who recognize this may take advantage of them and use them to further their own objectives.

Avoidance of Bullying

Bullying is a common occurrence in schools for children who have not yet formed a strong character. Children who are terrified of becoming victims of bullying may join groups or gangs where they feel safe and protected in order to get away from it all. However, joining those gangs can put the child under a lot of social pressure to do certain things or, in the worst-case scenario, conduct certain crimes, becoming delinquents, which can lead to a variety of other problems, such as going to juvie.

Want to Feel Cool

Coolness is a very important factor for teenagers, and these age groups are frequently concerned about it. As a result, in order to impress others and boost their social status at school, teens are often willing to modify their clothing, value systems, and even hang out with criminals in order to improve their level of coolness.

Humans Aspire to be Well-liked

We all want to be loved and valued as humans, especially children. However, this is a significant flaw that might be exploited by other children, especially if they know that the child comes from a broken home, where the child is not getting enough love or attention from their parents. If children try to please everyone, they'll have to give up a lot of their personality. As a result, they may become too weak to reject things due to peer pressure, and they may commit crimes or engage in other activities in which they do not want to be involved. The need for affirmation may make children subject to peer pressure and its negative consequences.

Hormonal Factors

When it comes to peer pressure, there may be hormonal concerns, especially for teenagers. Teenagers' hormone systems are complex, and hormone levels fluctuate often. As a result, teenagers are particularly prone to peer pressure, as their hormones may impair their capacity to appropriately appraise certain activities.

Bad Parenting

Parents have a significant impact on their children's mental development. If parents instil self-esteem in their children at a young age, such children are likely to be less subjective to peer pressure because they have established a strong enough character to value their own viewpoint over that of others. If the child's parents don't care too much about them, though, they're more likely to have low self-esteem, which might make them vulnerable to peer pressure and the consequences that come with it.

Religion

In the context of peer pressure, religion may also play a crucial impact. If the child grows up in a household where religion is very important, they may feel obligated to follow certain religious views even if they don't believe in them. As a result, religion may limit their ability to establish their own opinions since peer pressure is often too strong.

Cultural Values

Cultural values, like religious views, may play an important role in the development of peer pressure. If children live in a conservative atmosphere with stringent cultural rules that everyone is expected to obey from an early age, they may be pushed to take certain acts as a result of peer pressure and unconscious manipulation.

Personal Confusion

Teenagers in particular, may feel confused and lost in life. This personal confusion may also make them prone to peer pressure, as they may be desperate to find others who would support them. As a result, they may end up in gangs or other groups that utilize peer pressure to control them.

The Effects of Peer/Social Pressure
Changes in School Performance

Social pressure can have a big impact on how well the child does in school. For example, if the child starts hanging out with people who don't care about their grades, their own grades are likely to drop. Furthermore, if they engage in unlawful activities as a result of peer pressure, they may not have time to complete their schoolwork properly. Significant changes in school performance may thus be a sign of peer pressure and should serve as a warning to parents.

Behavioural Changes

Social pressure also causes significant changes in the attitudes of those who are affected. If the child hangs around others who have very different perspectives on life, for example, a child who believes that people are good, starts hanging out with another who thinks the opposite, their view may change over time. Social pressure has the potential to drastically alter children's perspectives on life.

Changes in Appearance

Teenagers who are subjected to social pressure may alter their physical appearance dramatically. This could include hair colour changes as well as piercings or tattoos. Parents should be concerned more or less depending on the change in physical appearance. At the very least, parents should pay close attention to changes in their children's physical appearance in order to discover early warning signs and respond appropriately.

Truancy

Teenagers who hang out with others who don't care about school, who despise their teachers, and who don't care about their future are more likely to stop going to school on a regular basis. Social pressure may thus lead to a drop in school attendance, resulting in a lack of knowledge and poor career chances in the future.

Bullying

Bullying in schools can also be caused by social pressure. Especially in schools with a large minority population, there is a good risk that some minorities will be bullied. Social pressure may worsen the problem since children may be forced to choose between being the bully and becoming a victim of bullying. Due to social pressure, children may engage in bullying others out of fear of being bullied themselves.

Drug Use

Drug usage is very frequent, especially among teenagers. However, while using drugs may be enjoyable at first, it can lead to drug addiction and the problems that come with it. If they hang out with people who use drugs, for example, there's a good possibility they'll try it themselves at some point. If they enjoy it too much, they may become drug addicts and have a difficult time later in life.

Who Children should Talk to When Experiencing Social Pressure

As children become older, they'll have to make some difficult choices. Some questions do not have a clear right or incorrect answer, such as whether you should play basketball or soccer. Other options need major moral considerations, such as whether to skip class, smoke, or lie to your parents.

Children facing social pressure should speak with someone they can rely on. If they're still feeling stressed, talk to a teacher, counsellor, parent, or a friend about it. It will be beneficial for them to talk out their feelings with someone they can trust and rely on. These persons can assist them in practicing saying no or learning to say no in new ways.

How can Social Pressure Affect their Adult Lives Later?

When we enter adulthood, we typically believe that the worst of our childhood experiences are behind us. But, whether we're teenagers or seniors, concerns about our appearance, the need to be liked, and even the propensity to do something just to fit in continue to affect us. Social pressure can follow children into their adult lives. Why do they still give in to others?

Everyone wants to feel like they belong, no matter who or what age they are. This means that family, friends, co-workers, other members of organizations to which they join (e.g., church), social media friends, and other types of media have an impact on them.

Because they were so easily influenced by others when younger, as adults they may find themselves still being pressured into doing things they are not comfortable with.

1. Drinking with friends on weekends since everyone else is doing it.

2. Working extra hours to maintain a lifestyle that allows them to keep up with their friends and family

3. Purchasing items that aren't necessary in order to keep up looks

They learnt somewhere along the way that they're wants and needs don't matter. This can occur as a result of poor parenting, in which they did not receive the unconditional love and protection that a child needs, and as a result, they now have 'attachment issues.' They were taught that they had to earn love and attention as a child, and now they do it as an adult by being 'people pleasers.'

Stories about Social Pressure
Scenario 1

Tandy, a 15 year old, was hanging out at the mall with her three friends. She was extremely excited to hang out with them, as she hadn't hung out with them outside of school for a couple weeks. They walked around the mall for a while, stopping to get something to eat and drink when they got hungry. They then went into a clothing store. Two other girls who were friends with Tandy's friends were standing by the earring rack checking out the earrings. They called them over. When they walked over, the girls were trying to make them steal an earring for them. They told them they wouldn't get caught. Tandy's friends told her that they did it the last time they were there, she should try it. She knew it wasn't right to shoplift but she didn't want her friends to think she wasn't cool. Tandy looked around to ensure no one saw her then dropped the earrings in her bag.

Scenario 2

Matthew was a soccer player, and he received a scholarship for a prestigious high school. He was new to town, and it was the first day of school. By the second period, he had already made friends with a group of guys. Everyone seemed nice enough and cool. He had a good time with them at lunch and wanted to spend more time with them, so when one of them asked him if he wanted to meet up after school, he said sure once he was finished with practice. When they met up, they all decided to chill behind the bleachers. Matthew noticed one of the guys pull out a cigarette and lit it. He asked him if he wanted one. He hesitated, thinking about how he could get caught and be suspended. However, not wanting to be deemed uncool, he accepted.

How to Deal with Social Pressure

Paying attention to their feelings and emotions. If something doesn't feel quite right, it probably isn't. The more aware they are of their emotions, the better they will be at recognizing them, being cool in stressful situations, and maintaining control.

Find a friend who will say no. It's difficult to be the only one who says no. Try spending time with a friend who is likewise willing to say no to skipping class or smoking a cigarette, and do something you both enjoy together. There is strength in numbers, and they might discover that they have more people joining them than if they went out for a cigarette!

Have a code that they can use to communicate with their parents. Something the child can tell their parents or text them to let them know they need to get out of a situation. Parents can contact or text the child to inform them that they must return home or that they will pick up the child.

Seek help from a responsible adult, such as a parent, teacher, or guidance counsellor. A trusted adult can listen to the child and provide ideas that might be effective in their situation.

How can Children Heal from Social Pressure?

Given the detrimental consequences of social pressure on adolescents and teens, it's critical for parents to help their children overcome this challenge. The following are suggestions on how to help kids heal from social pressure in a healthy manner:

1. To lessen the negative consequences of social pressure, schools should teach students about peer pressure and how it may affect their current and future lives. Children may be better prepared to resist social pressure and instead act in accordance with their own values as a result of this schooling.

2. Parents should help build children's self-esteem. It is also critical for parents to instil self-esteem in their children so that they are not overly reliant on other people's approval. Social pressure will be less likely to cause children to engage in criminal acts if they have enough self-esteem and know what they want and don't want to do.

3. Encourage the child to seek out positive interactions and find friends who will respect them and will not put them under undue strain.

4. Encourage your child's freedom and educate them to trust their instincts. Tell them that they won't be able to please everyone, and that's okay.

SOCIAL PRESSURE HELP
1- **KIDSHELPLINE (US)**
   Call 1800-55-1800

2- **CHILDLINE (UK)**
   Call 0800 1111

www.ingramcontent.com/pod-product-compliance
Lightning Source LLC
Chambersburg PA
CBHW071533080526
44588CB00011B/1655